CELEBRATING THE FAMILY NAME OF XU

Celebrating the Family Name of Xu

Walter the Educator

Silent King Books
a WhichHead Entertainment Imprint

Copyright © 2024 by Walter the Educator

All rights reserved. No part of this book may be reproduced in any manner whatsoever without written permission except in the case of brief quotations embodied in critical articles and reviews.

First Printing, 2024

Disclaimer

This book is a literary work; the story is not about specific persons, locations, situations, and/or circumstances unless mentioned in a historical context. Any resemblance to real persons, locations, situations, and/or circumstances is coincidental. This book is for entertainment and informational purposes only. The author and publisher offer this information without warranties expressed or implied. No matter the grounds, neither the author nor the publisher will be accountable for any losses, injuries, or other damages caused by the reader's use of this book. The use of this book acknowledges an understanding and acceptance of this disclaimer.

Celebrating the Family Name of Xu is a memory book that belongs to the Celebrating Family Name Book Series by Walter the Educator. Collect them all and more books at WaltertheEducator.com

USE THE EXTRA SPACE TO DOCUMENT YOUR FAMILY MEMORIES THROUGHOUT THE YEARS

XU

In the whispers of the ancient breeze,

The name Xu floats with timeless ease,

A lineage bold, yet calm as dew,

Rooted deep, forever true.

From mountain peaks to river's flow,

Xu's legacy continues to grow.

A bridge between the past and now,

A steadfast heart, a humble vow.

Through seasons' turn and ages' flight,

The Xu name glows, a guiding light.

With wisdom earned and dreams pursued,

Its strength in unity renewed.

Bamboo tall, unbowed, serene,

The Xu's spirit remains evergreen.

Graceful yet firm, its stance unique,

A voice of clarity when others speak.

In fields of gold or bustling streets,

The Xu family rises, its journey meets

New challenges, with courage high,

Reaching further than the sky.

Harmony blooms where Xu has tread,

A balance struck, where others dread.

A family bound by threads unseen,

Woven strong in every scene.

With every step, a mark they leave,

A legacy others can only perceive.

Through arts, through science, through paths untold,

The Xu name carves stories bold.

In every word, in every deed,

The Xu clan plants a lasting seed.

A name of pride, of quiet might,

Forever shining, day and night.

Through trials faced and victories won,

The Xu name rises like the sun.

Unyielding, steady, true to its core,

Its echo resounds forevermore.

So here's to Xu, a name so grand,

A heritage spread across the land.

In every heart, a spark anew,

A family cherished, strong, and true.

ABOUT THE CREATOR

Walter the Educator is one of the pseudonyms for Walter Anderson. Formally educated in Chemistry, Business, and Education, he is an educator, an author, a diverse entrepreneur, and he is the son of a disabled war veteran. "Walter the Educator" shares his time between educating and creating. He holds interests and owns several creative projects that entertain, enlighten, enhance, and educate, hoping to inspire and motivate you. Follow, find new works, and stay up to date with Walter the Educator™

at WaltertheEducator.com

www.ingramcontent.com/pod-product-compliance
Lightning Source LLC
LaVergne TN
LVHW052009060526
838201LV00059B/3930